MW00784660

AND LOVE SPEAKS

WRITTEN BY
J.L. BLAIR

ILLUSTRATED BY
MARK NINO BALITA

For Sandi.
This book is dedicated to and inspired by
your love, strength, and humor.

Illustrations and Cover Art by Mark Nino Balita
Typography by Qamber Kids

TODAY WE HAD A FAMILY MEETING.
IT WAS AFTER BREAKFAST WHEN WE WERE DONE EATING.
WE ALL SAT QUIET IN THE LIVING ROOM.
ME, MOM, DAD AND GRANDMA. MY BROTHER AND SISTER, TOO.

"WE HAVE SOME NEWS," MOM SAID AT THE START.
"GRANDMA IS SICK. THE NEXT FEW MONTHS MIGHT BE HARD."
I LOOKED AT GRANDMA, FROM HER FEET TO HER HEAD.
"SHE DOESN'T LOOK SICK TO ME," I SAID.

"I DON'T FEEL SICK, EITHER," GRANDMA CONFESSED.
"BUT I HAVE A DISEASE CALLED ALS.
IT MAKES MY MUSCLES STOP TALKING TO MY BRAIN,
AND OVER TIME THEY'LL STOP WORKING THE SAME."

ALS? THAT JUST SOUNDS LIKE SOME LETTERS.
"HOW DID YOU GET IT? AND HOW DO YOU GET BETTER?"
IT'S NOT THAT SIMPLE, MY FAMILY EXPLAINED.
AND SOON ENOUGH, THINGS WERE GOING TO CHANGE.

ALS is a sickness that starts with tiny clues.
Muscles might twitch or your legs feel hard to use.

Dad said, "It gets worse, though. You might feel scared.
At some point, Grandma may need a wheelchair."

"MY BODY ISN'T GOING TO GET ANY BETTER."
GRANDMA SAID, "ALS WILL BE WITH ME FOREVER.
BUT NO MATTER HOW THINGS CHANGE IN TIME,
I'M STILL YOUR SAME, GOOFY GRANDMA INSIDE."

I GAVE GRANDMA THE BIGGEST HUG I COULD SQUEEZE.
SHE HELD ON TO ME TIGHTLY. "BEN, YOU'RE SO SWEET."

"I'M NOT AFRAID OF ANYTHING. I'M BRAVE AS CAN BE.
I'M SORRY YOU'RE SICK, BUT YOUR ALS DOESN'T SCARE ME."

AFTER THAT, EVERYTHING WENT BACK AS IT WAS.
GRANDMA WAS STILL THERE TO MEET ME AT THE BUS.
SHE'D READ TO ME AT NIGHT, AND ON WEEKENDS, WE'D PLAY.
SHE EVEN MADE A CAKE FOR ME ON MY BIRTHDAY.

ONE DAY, GRANDMA WAS GETTING US A
DRINK AND A SNACK.

I WAS IN THE OTHER ROOM WHEN I HEARD
A LOUD CRASH.

I RAN TO THE KITCHEN TO FIND JELLY EVERYWHERE.
ON THE FLOOR, THE COUNTERS, AND A LITTLE IN GRANDMA'S HAIR.

GRANDMA STOOD THERE LAUGHING, SHAKING HER HEAD.
"MY HANDS COULDN'T HOLD THE JAR, AND I DROPPED IT INSTEAD."

IT WAS SUCH A STRANGE SIGHT, GRANDMA GIGGLING IN THE MESS.
WE MOPPED IT UP. "HOW ABOUT COOKIES, YES?"

LATER AT THE PARK, I BROUGHT A BALL TO THROW.
"CATCH, GRANDMA!" I SHOUTED, BUT SHE SHOOK HER HEAD NO.

"SORRY, BEN. TODAY I'LL JUST WATCH YOU PLAY."
I RAN FOR THE SWINGS WHILE SHE SAT IN THE SHADE.

WHEN I GAVE HER A HUG TO TELL HER GOOD NIGHT
I NOTICED HER ARMS DIDN'T SQUEEZE ME AS TIGHT.

"ARE YOU OKAY, GRANDMA? IS IT THE ALS?"
SHE NODDED HER HEAD. "BUT DON'T FORGET WHAT I SAID."

"EVEN THOUGH MY ARMS AREN'T AS STRONG AS THEY WERE BEFORE,
EVERY DAY I SPEND WITH YOU, MY LOVE GROWS MORE AND MORE."

SHE SMILED AND LEANED FORWARD TO KISS ME ON THE CHEEK.
"SWEET DREAMS, BEN," SHE SAID, BUT IT WAS HARD TO FALL ASLEEP.

THE NEXT MORNING, I'D MADE UP MY MIND.
GRANDMA HAD ONE BAD DAY. NOW SHE'D BE FINE.
MAYBE HER HANDS AREN'T SO STRONG, BUT THAT'S OKAY.
THERE ARE SO MANY OTHER WAYS WE CAN STILL PLAY.

We can play games. She can help me on my bike.
We can still sing and color and write.

"Hey, grandma, let's go for a walk!"
"Not today, Ben. How about we just talk?"

"Let's go to the park, to the zoo, to the store. All we do is sit and talk. I want to do more!"

But soon even talking got hard to do. Grandma showed me a sign so her love could speak, too.

AND THEN...
MOM BROUGHT SOMETHING NEW IN.

A TALL, BLACK WHEELCHAIR. I THOUGHT IT WAS UGLY.
IT HAD A MOTOR AND WAS BIG AND CLUNKY.

MOM HELPED GRANDMA SIT, HER
HANDS IN HER LAP.
FROM THE WAY IT LOOKED,
IT WAS LIKE SHE WAS TRAPPED.

"I KNOW IT'S SCARY, BEN, BUT JUST REMEMBER.
MY LOVE FOR YOU WILL LAST FOREVER."

"I WANT THINGS TO BE HOW THEY WERE BEFORE.
I DON'T WANT YOU TO HAVE ALS ANYMORE."

I WANTED TO SCREAM
AND YELL
AND CRY
AND KICK.
I DIDN'T LIKE THIS CHANGE ONE BIT.

MOM GAVE ME A HUG TO CALM ME DOWN.
"WE HAVE TO GET USED TO HOW THINGS ARE NOW."

GRANDMA'S LEGS AND ARMS AND VOICE WERE FINE
AS WE LAUGHED ALL THE WAY TO THE FINISH LINE.

WE ZOOMED PAST THE OTHERS. THEY WERE A BLUR.
GRANDMA WAS THE BEST DRIVER. YOU SHOULD'VE SEEN HER!

AND THE BEST PART WAS AT THE END OF THE RACE
WHEN GRANDMA GOT A TROPHY. SHE WON FIRST PLACE!

In the morning, I didn't feel as mad.
I wasn't as scared or even as sad.

Instead, I had an idea. I told Mom in secret.
I ran to my room to get what I needed.

"GRANDMA, WE WERE IN A RACE AND YOU WON.
IF YOUR CHAIR WAS LIKE THE RACE CAR, IT WOULD BE MORE FUN.
I BET IT'S FAST. CAN IT TAKE YOU OUTSIDE?
I CAN TIE ON YOUR SHOES AND WE CAN GIVE IT A RIDE."

"NOW WE BOTH HAVE CARS AND CAN RACE ALL DAY.
AND I CAN'T WAIT TO HELP YOU IN OTHER WAYS."

"WHEN YOU'RE HUNGRY,
I CAN MAKE THE SNACKS.

I CAN GET YOU A DRINK.
I CAN SCRATCH YOUR BACK.

I CAN COMB YOUR HAIR
AND GET YOU A HAT.

AND AT DINNERTIME,
I CAN FEED THE CAT.

SINCE IT'S HARD TO TALK,
I CAN READ YOU A BOOK.

I DON'T KNOW ALL THE WORDS,
BUT WE CAN BOTH LOOK.

IT'S OKAY IF YOUR VOICE IS TOO WEAK

LIKE YOU SAID, LOVE IS STRONG
AND LOVE SPEAKS."

THEY WERE RIGHT THAT EVERYTHING CHANGED.

WE CAME UP WITH NEW WAYS
TO HELP GRANDMA EACH DAY.

IT STARTED OUT HARD
BUT THEN IT GOT A LITTLE BETTER

BECAUSE MY FAMILY WAS THERE
TO GET THROUGH IT TOGETHER.

ALS Support/Resources

Amyotrophic Lateral Sclerosis (ALS) is a very challenging disease that affects all types of people: parents, grandparents, aunts, uncles, and friends. Of course, it also has an enormous impact on the children who love those who've been diagnosed with ALS. Children bring kisses, hugs, caregiving and joy to those living with ALS, but at the same time, those children may be experiencing confusion, fear, and worry as they watch the person they love face a scary disease.

And Love Speaks was written to help navigate those difficult feelings and conversations, to help children understand that their loved one with ALS is the same person inside, and to maximize quality time together. Just as Jamie wrote And Love Speaks to help children cope, there are others out there doing the same.

Hope Loves Company (HLC) is the only nonprofit in the United States with the mission of providing both educational and emotional support to children and young adults who have had, or currently have, a loved one with ALS. They offer resources to children and their families—at no cost—including, Camp HLC, Hugs of Hope care packages, scholarships, group shares, and so much more. You can learn more about HLC by visiting their website at www.hopelovescompany.org or calling them at 609-730-1144.

About the Author

Jamie L. Blair is a former teacher and librarian with a passion for children's literacy needs. With a USA Today Best-Selling series in her backlist, she knows good can be accomplished through books. And Love Speaks was written to help her own children understand their grandmother's ALS diagnosis, and by providing free copies to treatment centers and support groups across the United States, she hopes to benefit as many children and families as possible during their time of need. Proceeds from And Love Speaks goes back into the ALS community, providing more books and supporting ongoing research in hopes that someday,

we'll have a cure.

Acknowledgements

The production of this book was a team effort, and there are many to acknowledge:

My illustrator, Mark Nino Balita; My design team, Qamber Kids; My editor, Nicole Bailey; beta readers; the ALS community; Jodi O'Donnell-Ames - the founder of Hope Loves Company; and my partner, my family, and my friends, who all provide so much support.

Additionally, many contributed to bringing And Love Speaks to life through a public crowdfunding campaign:

Alberto, Amanda, Amber, Amy, Angie, Ann, Ashley B, Ashley R, Autumn, Ben, Cheyenne, Christina, Colleen, Diane, Elizabeth, Gary, Ginger, Heidi, Helen, Tia, Jacqui, Jake, Jay, Jenn, Jessica, John, Karen F, Karen W, Kathy, Kirstyn, Lexi, Lina, Lindsay, Lorenzo, Marcellus, Marijose, Martha, Melanie, Najla, Nancy, Patricia, Peggy, Rebecca, Rebekah, Roxanne, Sandra, Shawna, Steven, Sylvia, Tabatha, Tiffany, Tig, and Yvette

As of this writing, research and progress on an ALS cure have a long way to go, but there are many of us out there who want to help make things easier on the children who are impacted. I'm grateful for you all.

Printed in the USA
CPSIA information can be obtained
at www.ICGtesting.com
LVHW071320061023
760346LV00041B/7